# The Davids Inside David

Also by Sarah Wetzel

*River Electric with Light*
*Bathsheba Transatlantic*

# The Davids Inside David

by

Sarah Wetzel

Terrapin Books

© 2019 by Sarah Wetzel
Printed in the United States of America
All rights reserved.
No part of this book may be reproduced in any manner,
except for brief quotations embodied in critical articles
or reviews.


Terrapin Books
4 Midvale Avenue
West Caldwell, NJ 07006

www.terrapinbooks.com

ISBN: 978-1-947896-15-4
LCCN: 2018968581

First Edition



Cover art by Lukas Hahn
*Remnant*
Computer Generated Image

www.lukas-hahn.com

for my father

Raymond A. Wetzel

## Contents

| | |
|---|---|
| Reservoir Dogs | 15 |
| | |
| **I** | |
| Caravaggio Copying Caravaggio | 17 |
| Daughter Like Father | 18 |
| An Hour Too Late | 19 |
| Mostly Okay | 20 |
| To Replace See with Hear | 22 |
| Next Summer, Barcelona | 24 |
| Points of Reference | 26 |
| | |
| **II** | |
| Like St. Thomas | 29 |
| All of Us Running | 30 |
| Two Photographs of Winter | 32 |
| Someone Else's Dog | 33 |
| Drought | 35 |
| Then I Had the Idea | 36 |
| Of Myself a Basilica | 37 |
| | |
| **III** | |
| Regarding the Beauty of Cockroaches | 41 |
| Even the Monsters Were Good | 43 |
| The Marble Fawn and Other Anecdotes of Excess | 44 |
| The Outline of a Short Story | 46 |
| Neither Coming nor Going | 48 |
| The Year My Mother Died, 2009 | 49 |
| Miles from the Disaster | 51 |
| The History of the First Holy Door | 52 |

IV

The Davids Inside David                 55
My Father Draws My Face                  57
In David's Image                         58
The Next David                           59
The Male Gaze                            60

V

My First Face                            65
After the Flood                          66
Super Moon Blind                         67
The Day After You Left                   68
Never a Mary                             70
Woman as St. Bartholomew                 71
*Vanitas*                                72

VI

Original Idols                           75
The Crow                                 76
The Missing Century                      77
*James Hunter Black Draftee*             78
 In Rome's Protestant Cemetery           80
The Past as I Want It to Be              82
Transition                               83
A Mirror Is for Opening                  84

VII

A Case for Resurrection                  89
Ghosts of Sophia Loren                   91
Ambition                                 93
Descending Mt. Everest                   94

| | |
|---|---|
| Of Natural Causes | 96 |
| Breaching the Surface | 98 |
| La Porta Sacra | 100 |
| | |
| Acknowledgments | 103 |
| About the Author | 107 |

*Every block of stone has a statue inside it
and it is the task of the sculptor to discover it.*

—Michelangelo Buonanotte

*Sculpture occupies the same space as your body.*

—Anish Kapoor

## Reservoir Dogs

Praise Michelangelo for the purity he gave
the act—an adolescent David sculpted from stone.

He made the boy's face somber, as if David mourns
the giant's death, his left hand limply

still holding the slingshot. Looking up at him,
it's almost possible to believe in grace.

Yet, in a secluded corner of Rome's Palazzo Barberini,
I glimpsed something else—

Volterra's sixteenth-century painting of the same story
in which his David rides Goliath

like a horse, his hand raised not with a child's toy,
but with an enormous steel sword, his face

full of what I can only call ecstasy, fervent
as any boy's face, my nephew

watching for the tenth time his favorite
Tarantino film, anticipating the fists and knives, the ear

severed with a razor. Praise Michelangelo for not showing us
that boy, the one bent over his conquest

for a first kiss, tasting the flesh,
wanting more.

I

## Caravaggio Copying Caravaggio

It seems impossible to know which came first.
The darks are as dark as usual.
Christ's skin glows like the inside of a goblet.
The window behind me is open and people keep interrupting its light.
It's a Caravaggio but not nearly as weird.
All the men's feet seem proportional.
Their soles are too clean.
A fake is not a fake until someone notices.
The guard beating Christ seems incompetent; he's not putting his back into it.
Like the middle-aged man who bagged my groceries this morning at Kroger.
*I've just been released from prison*, he told me.
Beside the original muddle, another muddle.
It seems our Italian hero painted this scene not once but at least twice.
Two images of Christ and the men killing him.
We're supposed to see the differences even when there aren't any of significance.
I suppose disbelief requires too many scientific techniques.
But imagine the contrast of light and shadow in the actual version.
*There's not enough blood*, said the woman standing next to me.
Imagination isn't sufficient.
Or perhaps they're just getting started.

## Daughter Like Father

My father stands alone in front of the ocean
under a flattened sky, gazing
out over the gray expanse of water.
It's dawn and it seems from the window
where I watch him that there could be
no portrait more sad and lonely.
Seagulls wheel above the pier
where three fishermen cast their rods.
They are not the only signs of life—
the wind blows, whitecaps churn up
and resettle, a sailboat is drawn on and then
removed, sun-punctured clouds slide
across a slowly brightening sky.
My father could be the same monk
staring out into the German sea painted
by Caspar Friedrich two centuries ago.
The same wind reaches my window,
blows the curtain's transparent fabric across
my hand, small birds embroidered on its border
dart through my room. The tiny figure
of my father stands in front of the vast Atlantic
for almost forty minutes. When he finally turns,
he stumbles in the sand, falling
to his knees. I watch
as he slowly picks himself up, knowing
we will never speak of it.

## An Hour Too Late

When Sarah returns from Italy
where she'd spent long hours
on her knees, she finds
her husband's left hand on the table
still clutching
the key to the front door out of which
he must have just walked.

In this version of the story, she lifts
the hand with both of hers
as if a chalice brimming with sacramental
wine or a very old piece
of Venetian glass
fashioned into a pair
of hummingbirds, the light
through their cobalt-colored bodies
wavering across her face.

She writes long letters
to every known address and emails
every one of his friends she thinks
might answer her
as if she could stop herself dreaming
about hands
and how she has to give
at least this one back; the key he's holding
she'll keep, change the locks
and hide the knives.

## Mostly Okay

They are mostly okay. That's how the story
ends, how their story ends. My friend's
thirty-year marriage survived
her infidelities and business trips to cities
where her company didn't have business
as well as his two-year absence
that even the children don't mention.
There was the vacation to Spain
and the cab driver who stole their luggage
though the thief was so apologetic
they explain, when they retell the story,
that it was hard to be angry, all of us
laughing. The first baby, born
an epileptic, wore a crash helmet
to first grade and second grade
and died on a Wednesday at some point
between when the father read him
his favorite book, *How Many Trucks
Can a Tow Truck Tow*—tightening
the crash helmet strap under his chin—
and when his mother went to wake him
for school. He hated school
we all agreed. His younger sister who says
she doesn't remember her brother
wanted a son more than she'd wanted
a husband and when she couldn't
get pregnant, blamed him
though we all knew it was her body
that refused to hold on. The couple
went to Russia and adopted a baby boy
who they found out soon

had fetal alcohol syndrome. A year later
the sister divorced the husband. He's the reason
she doesn't drink. The child, I mean—
the sister doesn't drink because of the child.
There's always confusion about
who to blame. Though the boy, now seven,
is mostly okay. We agree he'll never
be a doctor or even
a poet, but the world has enough grief
without grieving
                    the loss of one more poet.

## To Replace See with Hear

hear without being blinded by my whiteness
by her redness and see-throughness
hear without skin
hear through sky through the clouds
hear the clouds shoving the sky open
hear the rain through the fog through night
hear drizzle
hear my body through my dress
hear through the eyepiece of a microscope
hear into a kingdom of algae
hear through the telescope
hear Syrius and Alpha Centauri not the skyline not skyscrapers
hear me without blinking hear me without sunglasses
I imagine your face without hearing it
I imagine your face after many years have passed
hear the inside of your eye hear eye to eye
the eye of the hurricane is never quiet
it's the electrical charge of the eye's resting state
in the dark I hear the shape of you moving
it's an afterimage but of what?
hear the light falling hear the light rising
I can hear through
hear in hear behind doors
hear the leaves and how they listen
hear the river and how it runs
                                        on and on and about nothing at all
hear sun and shadow and hear whirlpools and whirligigs

hear the lake and its shape around rocks
hear the bridge
hear a woman looking over her shoulder
hear as she steps onto it

## Next Summer, Barcelona

I'm in a bar listening to a woman
with a ring in her nose describe
her past summer. She'd walked what's called
"The Ignation Way," almost three hundred
and fifty miles of mountains, deserts, and plains
from the birthplace of St. Ignatius
in Spain's Basque country all the way
to the coast and Barcelona. It took her a month
and three sets of sneakers. She tells me
the one thing she found odd
was that most people on the trek didn't believe
St. Ignatius was a saint and some didn't even
believe in Jesus or God. Every night,
they'd meet in small groups and talk about
their feet, the next day's journey, the jobs
they'd lost and the people too, which towns
down the road had good showers and
cheap beds, the old man who slept outside
in a sleeping bag he carried under his arm
and kept to himself. What was his story?
The woman said she went because she needed
something difficult to do. And, really,
she shrugged, I had nothing else
going on that summer. My friend
who's teaching five classes at three
different schools to make rent said snidely,
*Wouldn't that be lovely.* My friend struggled up
from a low sofa to get herself a drink
and I knew she wasn't being sarcastic.
It would be—lovely, she means. But then
I suppose, I'm terrified too, terrified

that I'm wasting my life and won't finish
anything of consequence. That there's no
Barcelona and that there might not even be
a kind ending. My friend returned and we spoke
of films, an art exhibit that was opening
the next night. After a long while,
the woman with the ring in her nose said softly,
*I quit. I quit with only forty miles*
*to the coast. It was the blisters*
*and the rain. I just quit. I took a bus*
*to Barcelona. My father paid for my plane ticket*
*back to LA.* She laughed. *He doesn't let me*
*forget that I still owe him four hundred dollars.*
I said, *Shit,* but then thought of all the debts
I hadn't repaid. *You have to go back*
*and finish when you can,* my friend said,
*maybe next summer.* The woman said,
*I suppose so, yeah, definitely.*

## Points of Reference

Whoever loves the sea has nothing
but the horizon and movement

and doesn't have a point
of reference except for the constellations

which from a balcony at least
twenty floors up from the avenues

might be Mercury until Saturday
Venus from Sunday on.

Whoever loves the sea has the sound
of sand and its castles

tumbling, the enormous crashing
and imaginary bodies drowning in its moats

frightening my dog.
Women who love the sea have an idea

how close the other side is, how far away
and how many rows it would take

to reach the other shore where a woman
with a small dog and a book

is peeling an orange and wondering
from which direction I'll arrive.

*Sea*, she says.
                    *Hurricane. Earth.*

II

## Like St. Thomas

You've got to reach your whole hand
into the body,

open the wound wide,
tear flesh,

if you want
to place even one finger

on the other side of the canvas
which is a door, silent

like the silence I kept
by mother's bed that last month

listening to the rise
of breath, the burble

in the throat.
Death is what I bowed toward,

tensing as it darted away,
its voice opening and closing

me, showing its eyes
even as she finished, even

as the nurse
forced my fingers

from hers, forced me
from the hospice room

and into the waiting
room light.

## All of Us Running

> after *Freedom of Movement,* a video installation
> by Nina Fischer and Maroan el Sani

Consider a man running:
a man running through the center of Rome.
He passes the Colosseum, circles Circo di Massimo
running down and into and out of it
through the Arch of Constantine.
Consider him carefully.
His feet are bare
as he passes the triumphal arches.
Rewind and replay the footage
of a man running.
There are men in chariots,
men on horses, men on motorcycles
escorting him.
A man on a motorcycle paces him,
chases him. The man running
is shoeless, his legs, dusty.
His feet touch the ground
and then lift off.
He is aloft, held aloft
on a strong wind or a winch
through his back.
Consider a man running.
Consider the look on his face.
There is a dog.
Sometimes there's a dog.
There used to be many dogs.
He is aloft and running in air,
legs churning in air.
He is running for food for water for furniture

he is running for refuge for rope
he is running from machine guns and machetes
he is running from emptiness
toward an even bigger emptiness
filled with our sound.
Past the Protestant Cemetery, past
the Tomb of Priscilla, the soles
of his feet
strike and strike and strike the ground.
Consider a man running.
His shadow passes over the earth,
disappearing as if into it.

## Two Photographs of Winter

Where I come from there is a canoe
filled with white snow
                            beached
beside a river frozen over.

From a window
everyone I love is watching
                            a weeping
willow weep nothing
but icicles of iced leaves—

but somewhere not that far
                            a man hands
his infant through a break
in a barbed wire fence

barely large enough—
                            and the paw prints
of small animals I never see
crossing over.

## Someone Else's Dog

This is the thing—
on the way back from Plains, Georgia,
where my mother and her friend Marie
had taken me and Marie's daughter
to celebrate Jimmy Carter's inauguration
which I didn't care about
because it was 1977 and all I cared about
were books and the pink and white
writing desk my parents couldn't afford
and a little bit about boys. It was then
we ran over a dog or a fox—my mother
was never sure. She was driving
and those backroads of South Georgia,
which she sort of knew because
she grew up not far from Plains
which was the reason she and Marie
had worked on Carter's campaign, those roads
were very dark. I was trying to read
by flashlight while Marie's daughter stared out
the window, which is what she'd done
most of the trip, just as I'd barely glanced up
from whatever book I'd been reading.
It was then, perhaps a half hour
out of Plains, we felt an enormous thump,
my mother crying out, *a dog, I've hit a dog.*
Almost immediately Sheila, that was her name,
who no one in her grade, one behind mine,
much liked, became hysterical, sobbing
over and over *oh no, oh no, oh no.*
My mother pulled the car over
and she and Marie got out, emergency lights

blinking, to see if they could find the animal,
which they did. It was dead or as close
as she would let any of us find out.
*Stay in the car*, she yelled. I could hear
them talking about whether they should move it
farther off the road and if it
was a dog or a fox. We were never sure.
Anyway, after a few minutes my mother came
over to the car, to Sheila's side, pulled
that awful girl, still weeping, into her arms.
*Oh honey,* she kept saying, *I'm sorry,
I'm so sorry.* The thing is, it was then
I started crying too. *That poor dog,* I cried,
*we killed a dog,* as though it had been my dog
and not some dog none of us knew.

# Drought

I am waiting for a train the way
I still wait for rain

with its blue clouds and the stiff
breeze leading it.

Every year the rain arrives
later and the clouds' anxious cargo

already half-emptied. I am waiting
for a train the way I once

waited for my father
to step from a plane

to return from the country
my mother called war.

I raise my eyes as he walks toward me
across an undulating tarmac

as he did every night, waking me
from my nursery-school dreams.

I'm waiting for a train as if
it's the only route out

of this loneliness,
as if my father

for once in his life on time
is on board.

## Then I Had the Idea

there wasn't a good reason, the train left too soon
an email wasn't sent
the flowers never arrived
I wanted a baby and then I didn't
there was a reason
I tried with first one then the other
pretending becoming a way of becoming and then
about Curtis before he killed himself
that it might have been a little my fault
the phone didn't ring the phone rang but I wasn't there
I meant what I said
if you have to choose between me and another woman, *go*
I never wanted a baby not even someone else's
about alchemy about magic about men with unplaceable accents
about my mother's father about Steve about driving a car
the distance between a child's feet and the brakes
there is a lake in Rome that no one has named
there are many more hills than seven
there is a river with seventeen names, all of them mine

## Of Myself a Basilica

My body, a cathedral, my hair adorned
cosmati-style of stone salvaged from the ruins
of ruins, arrayed in circles and squares, octagons
of black and blood marble, my hips
and buttocks, coarse-crystaled and my waist
serpentine, circumscribed with mosaics, ribboned
in gold-layered tesserae. Hymns I invent, whistle
so that every one of the Twelve
must listen. My fingers neither small blocks
of rock nor measures of grain, the tips dipped
in water found at the gate, I trace a path
up one arm then up the other, place one
by one in my mouth. I taste not the wet
but the day's walk, the hour I spent in the sun
at a table in Piazza Farnese, the *No*
I kept giving the migrant from Mali, his arms
garnished with multi-colored beads, braided
with bangles. When he kept demanding
something, anything, I gave him two Euro
just to say *Yes*.

I admit I've been frightened, pouring
the penance of water, hand to hand, my mind
a church, its steeple, from which emanate
dreams of over-large animals, visions
of mammoths and saber-toothed tigers.
Forgiveness is an old man dressed
as a priest, who's waiting for someone
to wake him. Forgiveness is the old man
dressed as a gypsy, his lips to the ground. I want
to kiss both of them, either one of them. Yet no one's

mercy is really here, or even much pity. Just relics
and I won't turn what I did or didn't do
into something confessable. I scoop air
from under the gold *baldacchino*.
It's as much mine as anyone's, though I admit
I'm clutching an anchor while everyone else here
seems to be banging together their boats. Still
I refuse to regret my lies; they were done for love
of myself, which is, I suppose, a kind
of benediction. *Per favore*, the priest says softly,
but it's past dusk and what he means is
*I want to go home*. All I can give is another two Euro.
All I take is a candle for lighting the way out.

III

# Regarding the Beauty of Cockroaches

> after *Caixa das baratas (Box of Cockroaches)*, 1967,
> by Lygia Pape, acrylic, mirror, mummified cockroaches

The little boy says, *Those are real cockroaches.*

*They aren't "real,"* says his sister.

A small pool of fog appears and disappears in the glass case
  as the boy breathes.

Like them, I trust less and less in appearances.

*Why are they orange?* the girl asks.

The little girl keeps repeating the word: *mummified.*

The children circle the glass box, leaving their fingerprints.

The Portuguese word *baratas* derives from the Latin *blatta*:
  an insect that shuns the light.

When cockroaches first appeared, vast swaths of forest
  covered the earth.

Cockroaches now live in the Arctic.

Some live under water carrying a bubble of air within their bodies.

We call fallen leaves, litter. Many live in leaf litter.

*How does one stand / To behold the sublime?* Wallace Stevens asked.

*I think they're awesome,* says the girl.

I too believe the soul should stand in awe.

Cockroaches raised in isolation rarely leave their shelter
  and take longer to recognize mates.

So instead of asking, *How do I look?* ask me, *What do you see?*

Art breaks down the boundary between its object and life—

      this is the mummified remains of a forest, my father told me,

        holding up a lump of coal, before throwing it onto the grill

—and every now and again,

                feeds a small fire.

# Even the Monsters Were Good

And I was formless and empty
shaking
    a baby rattle that I loved
as much as a baby loves anything

and my mother read to me.
       My father read to me
from Vietnam
    recording Dr. Seuss stories
on cassette tapes
before he'd plan the day's

     defoliation of forests
     clothes burned from bodies

and their voices separated the dark
        from the light
and I wasn't afraid of the night.
Repeating their rhymes

I learned to say *sky* and *cloud* and *leaf*
and *bye, bye, bye*
    *what* but not *why* when I pointed
to the shadows.

# The Marble Fawn and Other Anecdotes of Excess

*after seeing* The Marble Faun (Fauna rosso) *in Rome's Capitoline Museum, Palazzo Nuovo.*

1.
Muscled calves and overworked thighs, neck thick with the weight of wineskins and ferrying baby goats. I thought the boy would be graceful or at least a little more delicate, although the cracks in the arm and back indicate he's been broken at least twice. His entire body, sculpted from red marble, seems to pulse with pleasure; though only his pointed ears, no doubt coated with soft fur, seem edible. The goat staring up at him seems drunk too, or at least too gay for a goat, his mouth laughing at something his shepherd had said. He's a shepherd, sure, but most of his sheep are long lost or eaten by wolves, taken easily by thieves, even his pipes, probably his ninth or tenth pair, the others left hanging on a tree's branch while their wine-blind owner tried to find home. Grapes grown and crushed, sugared and consumed too quick. But let's not regret what's already done. Pipe us a song, Animal-Boy, if you can remember one; we've been pretending you're not one of us, for centuries.

2.
I should have told Tina it was time to call her mother when she, nineteen years old and my student, said she thought she was pregnant and asked, her eyes staring into mine, *What should I do*? It was too late to teach her the ridiculous Italian word for *condom*—*preservativo*—and anyway she said it'd been an Italian and trying to convince one of them to wear one was, even old teachers know, not an easy task, especially in English. This was the same girl I'd taken to the pharmacy to buy something to treat a yeast infection. The same girl who

showed up smelling of beer two mornings of four though she'd, so far, submitted her homework on time and never been more than five minutes late to class excursions. I taught her how to say *pregnancy test* in Italian—*test di gravidanza*—and then bought her a three-pack even though I knew I'd regret it. After all, she was my favorite.

3.

But, she said, I wanted the dirty jokes and the small ears. I wanted a strong back and a tattoo on every appendage. I wanted his piercings, three in each ear and particularly the one through his tongue. I wanted the huff and puff and for him to blow my house in. I wanted the loud Italian music *Negrita* and *Subsonica*, and the cheap English beer. He was too poor for a whole joint, but he offered me half of what he had and didn't get mad when I took almost all of it. The Carrefour supermarket where he used to work had issued an arrest warrant after he stole the entire hind leg of a hog, uncut and stuffed in his bag. He said he didn't intend to keep it, but for god's sake, who takes so much *prosciutto crudo* and doesn't mean it? I paid for dinners and didn't mind, but I wouldn't let him take any photos of me naked. After I left Italy, I deleted even the ones with our clothes on.

## The Outline of a Short Story

A woman sits in a small cafe
holding a book she has yet to open.

She sees an ex-lover arrive
with someone else, take a table outside.

Of course, this is the same place
where she and he often met, remaining

for hours, reading each other's minds.
He's still a student, the same

backpack slung on one shoulder. She watches
as he takes out his phone

to show, she knows, photographs
of art installations he constructs

from broken plywood, the trash of strangers.
He has green eyes; his hair brushes

his shoulders. He leans close
to the woman beside him, gesturing

with one hand and she wonders
if he still lives with his mother.

And I sit at a small table, observing
the three of them, writing

a letter I'll never send to someone
I have yet to meet. Outside

it's beginning to storm, which is rare in Rome
even in winter and the tables

with their cheap white table clothes, tiny
coffee cups, fill with water.

Palazzo Farnese, closed for the season,
turns invisible. The man

and the woman he's with
rush inside. *It will pass soon*, he says, gently

wiping her damp face with a napkin.
The other woman sitting just behind them

writes it all down, word for word.

## Neither Coming nor Going

> after *Staircase in Capri* by John Singer Sargent

There is no beginning—only stairs
opening to the sapphire of a Capri sky, a tree's
leaves twining above white on white walls.
We don't see where it ends.

But when two Buddhists marry, do they promise
to be true beyond the day death parts them
and exactly how long is forever? If men loved
is the marker, I've lived

at least four lives. If jobs, more than eight
though the summer spent cleaning
the houses of people who couldn't remember
my name doesn't count, but if you count

every dog who greeted me in a doorway
I've lived seven. I refuse to be finished
and Sargent, who paid his bills
by painting portraits in which rich people

look taller and thinner than in
real life and one of a pale woman in a plunging
black velvet gown, preferred to paint *plein air*
landscapes and, in London, just days before

he died, wrote that if he missed any city
it would always be Paris, though he couldn't think
of one place he hadn't managed to visit
at least once in this lifetime.

# The Year My Mother Died, 2009

On the mornings my father wept
and there was a time when it was
most mornings, he cried
over yesterday's disasters,
the predictions that the stock market
would collapse further and
*how much more can we lose,*
the anchors on CNBC asking
over and over. He wept
over the bark of the neighbor's dog
locked up when the husband left
on business thinking the wife
would return the same night,
but she never did. Three days
later, the nonstop howls
finally brought the police, and the dog,
covered in shit, was so happy
to see a human face
that he leapt all over
the policewoman's legs.
On the mornings he wept,
I went through those dark hours
as though through yellow lights, my hand
hitting the car ceiling, hoping
I'd beat red and most times
I didn't. I made coffee and knocked
on his bedroom door until he turned
quiet because he hated to be heard
though how not to be heard
even over the plane crashes
and suicide bombings,

the AM hosts counting
the billions lost in overseas trading
and the two Wall Street bankers
who'd jumped to their deaths,
their wives weeping
on *Good Morning America*
and my father rushing out
to console me. Then we turned
on an old Western, where
the bad guys don't bleed
and the good guy doesn't always
get the girl, but even that,
we agreed, was a fine ending.

## Miles from the Disaster

Awake at 2AM I know that this is the end
of the vacation, the pleasurable

company I kept and the open tab
at the bar whose name I could never pronounce.

There is no black like the black
inside a night stripped of electricity, no silence

greater than that created by fingers
inserted deep in the ear

yet even the incessant thunder, the floodwaters
swallowing this Tuscan town can't drown

my heart's thrashing. There's no
swimming out, the bed taken by the current

of whichever river this is, ferrying
whatever boat that I've clambered into.

In the last few hours I've come to suspect
that even Italy can feel one stop before hell

like the corridor outside the cancer ward
wallpapered in tiny gold birds

their velvet bodies worn smooth by the hands
waiting and where I still hear

miles from where it happened
my mother laughing at the doctor's terrible joke.

## The History of the First Holy Door

it is unhinged and wrapped in white cloth
its two thousand pounds lifted and laid out
it is taken to the basement of the Vatican
it is stored in a dark room and never visited
it is stored in a dark room and forgotten
for safekeeping for interest for further investigation and posterity
it stands for ten years in a pope's chamber
fingers wet with saliva, he rubs the glowing feet of his own Mary
it is bought and sold seventeen times in secret auctions
it is bid on by women in veils and through video monitors
it is hung in the bedroom of a Chinese industrialist and his bride
they make love in its shadow
they strangle each other in its shadow
it is nailed open
its history is wiped clean from the Internet
not a photo not a line written of its openings and closings
it is melted down, its body poured into door handles and cups

IV

## The Davids Inside David

The David standing in the Galleria dell'Accademia is fake.
That David in Florence's Piazza della Signoria is as real as the real David.
Ten tiny Davids can be purchased for ten Euro or even for nine if you bargain.
A tiny David with a magnet in his back holds a picture of David to my mirror.
David's eyes are colorless but I remember them blue.
Savoranola's followers hammered David to dust just after Michelangelo finished him.
Michelangelo sculpted another one.
Allied bombs destroyed David in the Second World War.
Michelangelo, almost certainly, made many more Davids.
After visiting the museum, my friend said, *He's both more and less than what I thought.*
We were speaking of men and not statues of men.
Small Davids exist inside Davids seventeen feet high.
There are many known replicas of David. Queen Victoria received at least one.
Michelangelo's last words were—
*A Starry Night* is where? *The Mona Lisa* is where? *The Manneken Pis*?
I'm sick of all this posturing.
But without hair, without teeth, I am unrecognizable.
Without the color of my eyes. Without both of my arms.
Without which arm, am I most unrecognizable?
Patrick Stewart doesn't have a single hair on his body.
Tilda Swinton is, in fact, more beautiful.
A madman sliced off David's big toe. Thieves stole the fragments.

What if every Titian in the Uffizi is a counterfeit?

When they opened Michelangelo's tomb, they found a small notebook and a pencil.

Would you write something down?

Write it down in my own handwriting, so I'll believe it.

## My Father Draws My Face

Before leaving St. Peter's Square, I send my father
a postcard; on the front, a smiling Pope stands

beside Bernini's fountain; on back, a Vatican stamp.
As I write out his address, I know my father

is just waking up. He'll look at the clock, which is six
hours behind mine, to wonder if today

I'll phone him. He'll drink a cup of coffee or two
and, very soon after, he'll continue the portrait of me

that he started almost three years ago. As a model
he uses a photo from my wedding day,

though that man and I are long parted.
In the portrait, there is the Dalmation from my girlhood

and Rodin's *Thinker* and Michelangelo's *David*,
which in his idea of me exist in the same place.

There is love and rain in the portrait. A palm tree.
There is the trip to Prague we took together.

There is the one to Paris we didn't.
This is the same portrait that every child hopes

her father is drawing of her. Blue skies and grass.
The bankruptcy and missed birthdays. Even those.

And like most fathers, mine has little talent
for faces and he always gets the mouth wrong.

## In David's Image

I imagine Michelangelo's *The David*
in the dark, the air conditioner filtering out

the dust and microscopic particles of skin
and hair, the minuscule pieces

of his body. He is near death
or far from it, depending on how one feels

about centuries. He is perfect.
Even his overlarge hands have a purpose.

I imagine *The David* gone.
I imagine every version of him gone—

and then to see him without knowing
of him. To see not myself

in the mirror, to instead
see the mirror.  Yet look

how the face persists!

## The Next David

I want to be in Firenze's *Accademia*
when *The David* finally
                         falls, when he explodes
into white irreconcilable fragments,
dust to more dust
during what might be the eighth
maybe the eighteenth earthquake in Italy
in fewer than seven years.

It's malicious, but I want
to watch it. I want to be there
when the ground opens up
and Michelangelo's masterpiece leans
more than the fifteen degrees
he's allowed. When his right ankle
riddled with invisible fissures
                         gives way and gravity
takes him. I want to be standing

right next to Michelangelo's *Slaves*, the one
named *Awakening*, his hand
reaching through rock,
the rest of him still trapped
in his catacomb of marble.
I want to catch him
                         as he drops.
He'll be close to weightless.

## The Male Gaze

*He looks weak as a girl,* a tourist,
American and middle-aged, says loudly
to his wife and indeed Donatello's young David
wearing only knee-high boots and hat
resembles more a coquette
than a warrior. He stands lightly
one unmuscled arm resting
on slim hips, the other seeming incapable
of lifting the enormous sword
that hangs by his side. His hair
falls in ringlets beneath the hat,
which is encircled with flowers.
His belly is as round as a child's.
*Even you could take him*, the man
tells his daughter, ten
or eleven, as she pushes her glasses
back on her nose to gaze
upward. She and I peer
into David's face and his eyes
stare straight into ours.
This David, Donatello tells us, *is*
more woman than man
but only because this David knows
we're looking. He knows
that even as he walks across fields
toward his Goliath, as he weeps
over what will surely be
many losses, we're watching him—
*he's so pretty*, the girl says—

and, like a woman, this David
watches himself too. Like a woman,
the worst I could tell her—
*you, lovely girl, will be even prettier.*

V

## My First Face

For fifty-five years, Borges slowly went blind,
losing first grey and green, the small fonts, the leaf's
network of veins, then the difference between cerulean
and sapphire, between Chianti and claret. In the end,
it was every edition of Shakespeare, *love looks not with eyes,
winged Cupid's painted blind*. Five years later, everything
black, Borges said, *I'd always imagined that paradise
would resemble a library*. No one asked, *What, abandoned
to your labyrinth of darkness, do you imagine now?*

A man I married told me one morning,
*I don't think I love you*. We'd been married twelve years
though it took him another two years
to walk out the door. To be honest, I never loved him,
not even as I said *yes*. Yet I know, I'd still be with him
if he hadn't left.

Borges knew from a young age he would, like his father
and his father's father before him, become sightless. It's why
he read every book, he said, before he was fifty.
Why he refused to learn Braille and how
he could tell just by listening how many books
a bookstore held. It's how, even blind, he could draw
his own face—a scrawl without a mouth or eyes, a ball
of black string tossed on a white sheet of paper. The truth
is not always what's written down—

I loved that man and, if only a little, I love him still.

## After the Flood

Five days later and finally you write
*Are you safe, how high did the waters climb?*

I couldn't barricade the door with enough bags
I couldn't keep the rage from rushing up

Choke back the roots and the drowned cats
I couldn't light the last match, the one lamp

I couldn't stop the crazed dark
Guard the head that always finds the door's edge

Stop the flood taking everything from some
Forgive you, who it didn't even touch

Five days when I might have been dead
And then you ask, *Are you safe?*

I couldn't stop the rising up
I can't push the filthy waters back

## Super Moon Blind

We were driving to see the moon.
To the wedding of someone
we'd never met. We weren't sure
of the way so we followed the stars.
We followed a woman's voice insistently calling
out to us, guiding us. We said, *No, she's taking us*,
and we called it fortunate
that the Navy programmers and Air Force intelligence—
some of them our fathers and mothers—
developed the code, the ability
of our missiles, our nuclear-tipped rockets
fired from submarines and capable
of erasing cities the size of Rome and Tel Aviv
to find their cities, those other cities. We counted
ourselves lucky that it's always been
our generals calling the shots
and fortunate that at least this century
they haven't and not yet our cities. And now?
We are as close as we've been
and as close as we'll be for the rest of our lives
to the moon. We are lost in the desert.
We are lost on a highway that ends
at the edge of a country we will never escape
even under this cutthroat sky.

## The Day After You Left

What does it mean that I wanted
to unwrap the wool scarf double knotted
from her neck, place my mouth
to the chafed skin, then her lips
at least twenty years older than mine
to their vertical lines beneath the aubergine
hinting of waiting rooms and cigarettes?
What does it mean
that I wanted to touch
the tip of my tongue to hers?
She would taste like bitter orange.
The man—I suspect, her husband—
had stepped from the elevator
without looking to see
if she followed.
They'd ridden silently for twenty-four floors
except for the six words
he'd said to her the moment
they entered, *How could you be so stupid.*
It wasn't even a question.
She let him step out of the elevator
and stood examining her spotted hands,
the thin wedding band, as
the doors shut behind him.
She glanced only once at me
her eyes light green
though a lover might call them
emerald. The two of us
continued higher. And I wanted
to take her hand and lead her
to my hotel room door

left unlocked and the bed empty
because what I really wanted
was to bend her over the bathroom sink
wash her baby-fine hair—
shorn too short I thought
for winter—and dry the see-through
pink of her ears, and then,
kiss her as carefully
as the first time you kissed me.

## Never a Mary

> after Caravaggio's *Repentant Mary Magdalene*
> and *Rest on the Flight into Egypt*

I'm alone in the quietest corner
of the museum, both of Caravaggio's Marys
slumped in their chairs, drugged with something
given them. Their eyes don't even flicker.
In one painting, a black-winged angel
plays a violin, a dirge no doubt, old Joseph
holding the music, while the two women move
deeper into darkness. One of them clutches
the child, yet in her slumber, seems willing
to release him. I want art to be a signpost—
Caravaggio painted both his dead Marys
wearing the same hair, the same skin—
but maybe the artist was enamored more
with his red-haired model than with any
meaning for me. Maybe the guard
asleep in a corner could tell me.
I think of putting on my shoes to see
whether she's breathing. This might be
what it's like to be the last woman in the hold
of the last spaceship circling the dead earth.
All of the whores and saints, all of the secret
police, long buried. And the child, his eyes
wide open and waiting, knowing
he can't trust me
                            to catch him if he falls.

## Woman as St. Bartholomew

I'd never seen a woman carry her own skin,
didn't know it was even possible
to hold the face, its folds

and demonic hollows bearing
no resemblance
to the woman holding them

even though she'd worn them forty-five
and more years. I didn't know
they were mine until someone

handed them back to me,
the fleshy parts, collected and counted
though even gathered they weighed

but a few grams, even less
than a silk dress, an 18-carat
gold-plated bangle. I couldn't see

how I was supposed to love
the worst of it. I didn't yet know
a woman carries

her own knife. that while she's trying
on shoes, reading a magazine,
brushing her hair, she's practicing

how to cut
her own skin, that I'd only imagined
I'd be stronger.

*Vanitas*

The world keeps testing me.
The lemons falling one by one on the balcony,
the dead leaves from my neighbors' trees gathering
in small piles in its corners.
A young pigeon plucking down
from its own body. It's so hot I imagine
his self-mutilation as a form of defiance
though the red-tipped feathers—
tumbling like tumbleweeds down the film set
of an old Western starring John Wayne,
the one where the kidnapped girl
doesn't want to be found—
tell me that something's not right.

Some of us see signs. Some of us
live in the past. My talent lies in painting
and pretending, walking barefoot across
drought-stricken lawns after midnight. Tonight,
I gather the rotting lemons,
the leaves, the soft blood-tipped feathers
and the body of the half-naked bird.
When the neighbors' lights go off,
when they've barricaded themselves
behind doors, I climb their railing
and arrange what remains
into, what I like to call, still life with pigeon.

VI

# Original Idols

    after Ercole Drei's sculpture *Eva e il serpente*

This woman is no serpent's sucker.
You can tell by the plane of her stomach
she's nobody's mother.
This woman offers her lips to him
because she wants them more
                              than bee bitten.

And her indifference to her own nakedness?
It's never been different
especially not now
when her body's been shared
thousands of times over sixty-six centuries.
With her right hand she opens
                              his length,
turns his green and gold corpse
into slippers, his head, a broach, then runs
a chain through his eyes.

Though I can tell that, like me,
she's only pretending to fit in
to a place where she can't have
a permanent address.
                      She flays him.
She flies him. I practice the look in her eyes.
Look how she wears him.

## The Crow

I refuse to give in, as I refuse
the tin cans and wailing of the child

two floors up, as I refuse this morning's
televised car crash, the volume still reaching me

at the bath's bottom. This dark din,
useless as three baths in a day, useless

as the stuttering static of the man
paralyzed, his wheelchair capsized

into the crowd exiting last night's symphony,
his guttural rage. A crow flies

through the house, which crazes my dog.
Underneath the water, I listen

to his muffled barking, the crow
flapping from couch to kitchen chair

and into the sliding glass door.
The dog, the crow inside my mind.

Once, the dog almost had him.

## The Missing Century

My neighbor Helen was in the hospital two weeks
with a broken hip. She lives alone and has very good insurance.
It took her seven hours to reach her phone to call for help.
I only found out when she returned.
I have got to start paying attention.
One time I joked to a friend that the only way I knew Helen
was still alive was that her newspaper appeared
at her door between 7 and 9AM
and by mid-afternoon, it disappeared.
M calls me even when I tell him I'm busy.
I call D and K and M every day. I call my father
every forty-eight hours. There are many ways
to go missing. For three days, I didn't notice
the newspapers piling up. For another ten days,
I didn't notice that newspapers didn't arrive.
The pipe breaks in the back of the refrigerator
or the washing machine and water spreads over the wood floors
like the soft body of a prehistoric octopus
lifting and learning the ways that wood moves when wet.
I offered to bring her groceries but she said
she'd ordered enough to last at least a week.
It takes a lot to disappear but just a little to go missing.
The body can go without food for three weeks,
water for three days. The body can barely survive
three minutes without air. Plastic bags
come with a warning for children.
Twenty-three-hundred people go missing
in America each day. Two things to notice:
there is a giant plastic bag over the head of our century
and we're forgetting to breathe.

## *James Hunter Black Draftee*

> after the painting by Alice Neel

Every portrait, every painting is a death mask,
the whole world of faces, a cemetery
and what of James Hunter, black draftee
who in 1965 sat for his portrait just once
before being shipped out or perhaps he fled
north, but wherever he went

he didn't come back. Not even to Harlem.
His name is not on the Vietnam Memorial.
We've looked, I've looked.
I asked my father, *Are you sure every death
was recorded?* I was five
the first time I saw my father cry,

holding a letter that said his best friend
had died from a gunshot at close quarters
not in Saigon, but stateside. His name
isn't there either, though, my father said, *It should be.*
And I look at the portrait of James,
unfinished, in which

he's always twenty-one, maybe twenty-two,
one of three or, let me guess, four children, all
the rest girls. His eyes stare to the left
perhaps out a window. He's exhausted
or just tired of sitting so long
and so still, which seems a beginning

to let go, a complicity with death and that
Alice Neel never painted
his right hand, his left hand
raised to his dark face, his clothes only
a sketch as if he's already half gone, half ghost.
But in 1965, he was alive

and sitting in a chair in a small house in Harlem
and in Saigon, my father was holding
the hand of his best friend.
Both of them are no more, if James ever was.
Like the face of a first love appearing
in a crowd and then gone.

## In Rome's Protestant Cemetery

They are here. All of them: Gramsci,
Isabella Roselli, and John Keats,
the vagabonds and petty criminals, the girl
with the corsage on her wrist.
They are here. Their loneliness and love,
the heartache and the jealousy, my friend
who was the first man I loved, dead
and now belonging to no one. He's here
at the edge of a dock, one foot
on the top rung of the ladder, entering or
emerging from a body
of water, Lake Lanier,
I remember. His chest bare, his hair
gleaming in late August sun. He's about
to look up and beckon me in.
All of them. His mother and mine
and the boy he still is, waiting
to open the gate though the headstone
is plain, his middle name
the same as my father's, here
in a shoebox, in a box with the graves
of the others, here in photographs, a pot
of red beans and rice, chicken noodle soup
still simmering, a book of recipes
he's writing. *Do you think he sees us?*
his mother once asked me. He sees us.
All of them reaching for the hand
of Michelangelo, his languid Adam
painted on the Sistine Chapel ceiling
waiting for a touch of consciousness
and Eve, already there and wrapped

in the maker's arm. She was never
an afterthought. They're here on a sled
pulled by a pack of strong dogs,
a bouquet of balloons tethered
to the belt of a child, the wake of a speedboat
they're riding rocking the dock
and every footstep I've taken, theirs
beside mine.

## The Past as I Want It to Be

                    It's not just a magician's trick—
everything that disappeared
is still there
            isn't it?—
the iris opening wide, the eye
and then flower, the white horse mounting
                        another white horse
surrounded by a white fence
                  the way you looked at me
one eyebrow raised.
*Let's take a photo*, I said, even as you
shook your head *no*.
              Let's not.
Hello memory. Goodbye.
                      I can still hear
        the horses moving against
each other, smell
their wet grassy breath
              feel your hand on my throat
and as I turn
the white horses become spotted,
the irises, rhododendron.
                I remember you.

# Transition

>after seeing the paintings of Giuseppe Arcimboldo
>(1526-1593)

A small white fish swims through my mind—
a clump of undissolved vitreous gel
floating at the back of the eye
or like a dream that casts a shadow
on the retina, a crustacean
with its myriad legs as eyelashes.
*Fire, Water,* and *Earth* in Vienna and *Summer.*
*Spring, Fall,* and *Winter* in Rome.
*Air* was mislaid
between Prague and Paris. Strangeness counted
at least in the sixteenth century
if only with the aristocrats
who demanded some sort of reassurance
that it wasn't ending. Yet even now
there's an ambiguity occurring
in the middle of any ritual. You said you loved
the word *liminality,* which in Latin
means threshold.
We are all getting older
and like that          it was ending.

## A Mirror Is for Opening

With a damp cloth smelling of crushed
flowers, I remove the day's camouflage, my lips
I strip, expose the nose to marrow.

Beneath the bathroom's fluorescence emerges
time's sentence—furrows of forehead
and lips, my lashes' long hours, ligaments

of neck. Small broken capillaries appear
like question marks. The mirror is an unblinking eye
*or a door,* my mother was fond of quoting;

*a mirror is a door through which one
sees death,* she'd say, her face, cancer-thin, peering
out from spoons and newly cleaned bed pans.

A woman, I'd once read, is accompanied always
by her own image of herself. While she is walking
or weeping at the death of her mother,

a woman also watches herself walk
and weep. *I'm finally back to the weight I was
when your father and I got married,*

my mother had laughed. Yet in my mirror
I don't see only myself walking
and weeping. I see my mother—dear God,

she is beautiful—and I am looking in
that door,
        huge and hypnotic as my childhood's, because,
oh Mother, where else is there to look?

VII

## A Case for Resurrection

> The catacombs beneath Rome's Our Lady of the
> Conception of the Capuchins Church are decorated with
> the remains of almost 4,000 unnamed Franciscan friars.

This might be what Nabokov meant when he said art
is equal parts beauty and pity—six vestibules
of ulnas and humerus, hundreds of skulls architected

into arches, eyes overflowing with broken
bits of their own bodies, Baroque-style chandeliers hung
of human collar bones while below a group of six men

dead for more than three centuries sleep
still dressed in rough-woven robes, perhaps dreaming
mosaics of vertebrae leaves and petals

fashioned from hand bones, thousands of hands
formed into thousands more flowers and,
in the middle room, a mobile, which seems imagined

by one of Calder's forefathers, tinkles
with what it took me a few minutes to realize
are men's ribs. In all, there are five-and-a-half rooms

festooned with what remains of those friars' lives, lives
filled with baby teeth and little brothers, hang-
nails and heart attacks, their mothers long buried.

When no one was looking, I reached through
the protective wire mesh, ran fingers around a man's
empty eye socket. My hand came back coated

with what might have been dust but surely
contained a trace of what he'd been, his pain
and penance as well as our common hunger.

In the seventeenth century, the Catholic Church
excavated all these forgotten friars, piled
their corpses haphazardly into three hundred carts

drawn by three hundred donkeys. Then some
thirty years passed while someone, and no one
is sure who, arranged the remains into what

I have to call fantastic. Mosaics of mandible flowers,
the wall a chessboard of fleshless faces overlooking
a fibula table, femur and shaved tibia shaped

into what looks like a clock stopped just around
the time clocks were invented, wall hangings
of pelvises metamorphosed into flocks of prehistoric

birds as if the birds' spines suddenly remembered
they'd once carried wings, and at corridor's end,
a painting of Jesus, his hands on Lazarus.

# Ghosts of Sophia Loren

Half-awake yet still sleeping, I'm haunted
by thoughts of my mother

to whom I had never paid much attention
when she was alive. It's as if

I'm seeing her for the first time:
the month she lay in bed, her body

swollen with rheumatoid arthritis or lupus
or scleroderma or something

the doctors weren't sure of, the finger
she would press into her own flesh,

its indentation remaining long
minutes afterward; how she'd take

a tiny loud first sip from every beverage
as if testing its vintage, the floppy straw hats

she favored, the strappy sandals
she purchased and then would take back

feeling guilty for wanting something
so delicate; how when she walked

her hips swayed like Sophia Loren's,
my father once said; and how she'd spend

an hour or more browsing
the book section at Walmart, reading

the last few pages of the paperback
romances she might buy, as if

every ending weren't the same, *but some,*
she'd explain,
                      *are happier than others.*

## Ambition

I wanted to tell the woman at the party
that I knew the truth—
she didn't adopt her dog from a kill shelter,
which is what she was telling a group of us.
I held my tongue for fear of appearing petty.
We all want to be better than we are.
Yesterday, my sister called and asked for money.
At first, I told her no.
But she'd received the third notice from Georgia Power
so I paid her $700 electric bill though told her
never again, unless her husband got a job, any job.
I cc'ed him on the email.
He wrote back, *You're an awful person*
with a mixture of rage and bitterness I could hear
even on the screen. Still, this time
I meant it. I overheard the woman at the party
tell her friend they'd actually purchased the dog
from a breeder in upstate New York.
*We spent so much money, we could have adopted
a baby from China.* I found her statement funny.
I want to be better. I want to save a dog, to save
my sister. I want to tread lightly on this world without
leaving footprints or too many
plastic wrappers. I want to see Singapore
and Vietnam, to spend a summer in Italy writing
short stories and a sonnet or two.
Learn to tango and foxtrot equally well.
I want to be good.
I want to write one poem so perfect
that when I'm dead, a stranger will pin it to the wall,
perhaps even claim it as their own.

## Descending Mt. Everest

You are eight times as likely to die
coming down from Mt. Everest as you are
ascending its summit. You leave too late.

You underestimate how long it will take
to cross the southwest face, choosing
what you think is the fastest route.

Last spring, when two climbers, descending
toward base camp, passed the man sprawled
in the snow, they declared him dead.

*Divorce him*, my father said, when my husband
and I separated for the second time.
*I never liked him anyway.*

A day and a half later when the not-dead man
stumbled off the mountain
into the middle of what he thought

was a field of blue rocks, but was instead
tents and salvation, he said, *On the way up
the wind had been at my back*. That's how he knew

in which direction to walk—
straight into it. Standing on the summit,
you think, I've done it. Everything else

will be easy. Yet you rarely carry enough oxygen.
You don't read the sky right.
You ignore the gathering clouds. You think

all I have to do now is be happy.
But the hard part is getting back down
without dying, not to mention,

convincing your father
that what he meant to say was: *keep going.*

## Of Natural Causes

The first elevator opens and a paramedic
pushes out a stretcher, a body

wrapped head to toe in white tied to its bed.
Her face is covered.

The second elevator opens and a second paramedic
pushes out a stretcher, a body, slightly bigger

wrapped head to toe in white tied
to its bed. His face as well.

*Didn't their dachshund die only last month?* I ask the doorman.
Trees are planted outside but haven't taken root.

Something like the holy spirit hovers over them.
Something like the snow that pours over Mt. Everest's peak

pours over me too. There is never enough
oxygen, especially on the ground floor.

When my grandfather finally died,
I was happy that my grandmother outlasted him.

It felt like an answer to something I didn't know I'd asked.
Something like providence.

In the corner of the church, the children would whisper
to invisible friends with names like George or Alexandria.

Something like the holy spirit pours me over the ground
like the ground outside and all broken up.

Through the sheets their bodies vibrate with the beds' motion.
The lights of the ambulance ignite.
*Goodbye George.     Goodbye Alexandria.*

## Breaching the Surface

And the thought came to me that the person
on the other end of the phone
into which the woman on the park bench
next to me was speaking so frantically
was no longer there.
                      That he'd carefully
set down his phone on a small table
and left the room.
                      I see him walk out
the door of his weathered one-bedroom
bungalow, take a path that leads through
some low dunes toward the ocean.
The sun is already half-setting.
A breeze blows in from the water
and small waves lap the sand.
The tide is low and tidal pools pock
and waver in the waning light.
A few others are already there, staring out.
They stand silently watching
the red ball descend.
                      On the horizon,
a blue whale breaches the water's surface, twisting
its astonishing body into the air.
Then another.
                      In the house behind him,
the woman on the other end of the phone
continues to speak quickly, her words
a soft whirr like a helicopter's blade
in the distance. From the phone
on another table, a man's murmur.

From a third and then a fourth, voices
speak urgently
                    into the empty air.
What I'm trying to say is
you are not alone.

## La Porta Sacra

Right now, I am walking
through one of Rome's four sacred doors

wearing a backless dress as though it's a sin
I've committed. The hands of Jesus

lower, tired and worn
smooth by the grasps of the grieving

and aggrieved, his face wetted with sweat
from our fingers. Who can *not* touch him?

There is nothing more true—
the holy door is narrower than expected

and off-center, a narrative
of red and white light in the window, inside

an icebox filling with feverish
bodies—forgiveness

never finishes. Everything pours forth.
The fountain its meaning. Paintings

their history. Books, their words and white
spaces, and even the stone walls frescoed

with saints, their laughter and lies. We seek it—
the silence, overflowing with smells

of red beans and rice, lamb
sausage, and butter-lathed biscuits. A last meal

someone I loved cooked
before leaving me. I am walking through

each of Rome's four sacred doors opened
for sinners and every sinner better

than me. But I don't want forgiveness.
I don't even want to forget.

I see now—I want it all
to come rushing back.

## Acknowledgments

Grateful acknowledgment to the editors of the publications in which the following poems first appeared, at times in earlier forms.

*Barrow Street:* "Someone Else's Dog"
*Diode:* "Breaching the Surface," "Descending Mt. Everest"
*Duende:* "Daughter Like Father," "My Father Draws My Face," "My First Face"
*8 Poems:* "Original Idols"
*The Ekphrastic Review:* "The Marble Faun and Other Anecdotes of Excess," "Never a Mary"
*Forge:* "Solace"
*Free State Review:* "The Past as I Want it To Be," "Vanitas"
*Gravel:* "All of Us Running"
*Harpoon Review:* "Caravaggio Copying Caravaggio"
*The Indianapolis Review:* "The History of the First Holy Door," "The Male Gaze"
*Matador Review:* "After the Flood," "The Next David"
*Quiddity:* "Even the Monsters Were Good," "Super Moon Blind," "Two Photographs of Winter"
*Softblow:* "The Missing Century," "Then I Had the Idea," "Transition"
*SWWIM:* "Ambition"
*Tishman Review:* "Points of Reference"
*The 2River View:* "The Crow"
*Valparaiso Poetry Review:* "Ghosts of Sophia Loren"

Thanks also to The American Academy in Rome, where many of these poems started, and to The American University of Rome, which gave me a reason to continue them in the city I love. I am grateful to my father, Raymond Wetzel, and friends Timothy Liu, Karen Uhlmann, Marcela Sulak, Jane Medved, Dara Barnat, Michael Ahn, Diana Delgado, Sivan Rotholz Teitelman, Jorge Novoa, J. Mae Barizo, and Karen Alkalay-Gut for their careful attention and support. I also want to extend my special thanks to my editor Diane Lockward for her encouragement and the opportunity to share these poems in this book.

And finally, I want to thank Mike Jehle whose love has made all of this feel new again.

## About the Author

Sarah Wetzel is the author of *River Electric with Light*, which won the AROHO Poetry Publication Prize and was published by Red Hen Press in 2015, and *Bathsheba Transatlantic*, which won the Philip Levine Prize for Poetry and was published by Anhinga Press in 2010. She is a PhD student in Comparative Literature in the CUNY Graduate Center and teaches creative writing at The American University of Rome. She holds an engineering degree from Georgia Tech and an MBA from Berkeley. She completed an MFA in Creative Writing at Bennington College in 2009.

www.sarahwetzel.com

www.ingramcontent.com/pod-product-compliance
Lightning Source LLC
Chambersburg PA
CBHW020144130526
44591CB00030B/201